Great National Soccer Teams / Grandes selecciones del fútbol mundial

MEXICO / MÉXICO

José María Obregón

English translation: Megan Benson

PowerKiDS press

Editorial Buenas Letras™
New York

Published in 2010 by The Rosen Publishing Group, Inc.
29 East 21st Street, New York, NY 10010

First Edition

Editor: Nicole Pristash
Book Design: Julio Gil
Photo Researcher: Jessica Gerweck

Photo Credits: Cover Omar Torres/AFP/Getty Images; back cover Bob Thomas/Getty Images; p. 5 Jaime Razuri/AFP/Getty Images; p. 7 Victor Decolongon/Getty Images; p. 9 Popperfoto/Getty Images; p. 11 Keystone/Getty Images; p. 13 Daniel Garcia/AFP/Getty Images; p. 15 Laurence Griffiths/Getty Images; pp. 17, 21 (right) Lutz Bongarts/Bongarts/Getty Images; p. 19 Jonathan Daniel/Getty Images; p. 21 (flag) Shutterstock.com; p. 21 (left) Allsport UK/Allsport/Getty Images; p. 21 (middle) Marcus Brandt/AFP/Getty Images.

Library of Congress Cataloging-in-Publication Data

Obregón, José María, 1963-
  Mexico = México / José María Obregón. — 1st ed.
    p. cm. — (Great national soccer teams = Grandes selecciones nacionales de fútbol)
  Includes index.
  ISBN 978-1-4358-2497-3 (library binding) — ISBN 978-1-4358-2498-0 (pbk.) —
ISBN 978-1-4358-3234-3 (6-pack)
  1. Soccer—Mexico—Juvenile literature. 2. Soccer teams—Mexico—Juvenile literature. I. Title. II. Title: México.
  GV944.M6O37 2010
  796.3340972—dc22

                                    2009000479

Manufactured in China

CONTENTS

CONTENIDO

Mexico's national soccer team is one of the most skilled and most talented soccer teams in the world. Mexico has won the FIFA Confederations Cup once and the CONCACAF Gold Cup **tournament** four times. In 2005, Mexico won the FIFA U-17 **World Cup**.

México tiene una muy buena selección de fútbol. La selección de México ha ganado la Copa Confederaciones FIFA en una ocasión y el **torneo** de la Copa de Oro CONCACAF en 4 ocasiones. Además, en 2005, México ganó la **Copa del Mundo** para menores de 17 años.

Giovani Dos Santos (left) and Ever Guzmán celebrate during the U-17 World Cup in 2005.

Giovani Dos Santos (izquierda) y Ever Guzmán celebran durante la Copa del Mundo Sub-17 de 2005.

Soccer is a very popular sport in Mexico, and fans gather in large numbers to watch the games. Mexican fans call the national team *el Tri* because the players wear the three colors of the Mexican flag. Those colors are green, white, and red. "El Tri" means "the Three" in Spanish.

El fútbol es muy importante en México y se vive con mucha pasión. Los aficionados mexicanos asisten en grandes cantidades a los partidos y apoyan con todo a su selección, a la que llaman el Tri por los tres colores de la bandera mexicana, verde, blanco y rojo que utilizan en su uniforme.

This young fan is shown wearing the colors of el Tri.

Este joven aficionado muestra su apoyo por el Tri.

7

The Mexican national team has a long history in the World Cup. The team has played in it 13 times. In 1930, Mexico played in the first ever World Cup game. The World Cup has also been held twice in Mexico, in 1970 and in 1986. In both cups, el Tri reached the quarterfinals.

México tiene una larga historia en la Copa del Mundo, en la que ha participado en trece ocasiones. En 1930, México jugó en el primer partido de la historia del torneo. Además, México organizó el torneo en 1970 y en 1986. En ambas ocasiones, el Tri llegó a cuartos de final.

A Mexican player (right) tries to block a shot during the World Cup Mexico 1970.

Un defensor mexicano (derecha) trata de bloquear un disparo durante la Copa del Mundo, México 1970.

9

Two of Mexico's players have made world soccer history. Antonio Carbajal was the first player to play in five World Cups in a row. Claudio Suárez had 178 caps. In soccer, caps are appearances with the national team. This puts Suárez in second place on the list of players with the most caps.

Dos jugadores mexicanos han hecho historia. Antonio Carbajal fue el primer jugador de la historia en jugar cinco copas del mundo seguidas. Además, con 178 convocatorias, Claudio Suárez ocupa el segundo lugar en la historia en número de partidos jugados con una selección nacional.

Mexican goalie Antonio Carbajal is shown here training in France in 1961.

El portero mexicano Antonio Carbajal entrenando en Francia en 1961.

11

One of Mexico's current players stands out among the rest. **Defender** Rafael Márquez is a good example of the skill and talent that Mexico's players have. Márquez is one of the best defensive players in the world. He makes it very hard for the other team to get the ball past him!

Un jugador mexicano destaca por encima de los demás. El **defensa** Rafael Márquez representa muy bien la habilidad y el talento de los jugadores mexicanos. Márquez es uno de los mejores defensas del mundo. Es muy difícil pasar el balón por la zona donde juega Márquez.

Rafael Márquez cheers after scoring a goal during the World Cup 2006.

Rafael Márquez celebra tras anotar un gol en la Copa del Mundo 2006.

In 1999, Mexico won the FIFA Confederations Cup. In a very **exciting** match, Mexico beat Brazil in the final game after scoring seven goals. Cuauhtémoc Blanco was the best scorer in the tournament with six goals under his belt. He scored four of those goals in a single game!

En 1999, México ganó la Copa Confederaciones FIFA. En un **emocionante** partido en el que se anotaron 7 goles, México derrotó en la final a Brasil. Cuauhtémoc Blanco fue el líder de goleo de la copa con 6 goles anotados, 4 de ellos en un mismo partido.

Cuauhtémoc Blanco's great skills helped Mexico win the FIFA Confederations Cup in 1999.

La habilidad de Cuauhtémoc Blanco ayudó a México a ganar la Copa Confederaciones FIFA en 1999.

15

Mexico's most famous player is Hugo Sánchez. Hugol, as he is known, played from 1977 to 1998. He scored more than 400 goals in his career. Hugol was very successful when he played in Europe, too. In Spain, he was named the best scorer five times.

El jugador más famoso de México es Hugo Sánchez. Hugol, como se le conoce, jugó de 1977 a 1998 y anotó más de 400 goles en su carrera. Hugo Sánchez tuvo mucho éxito jugando en Europa donde fue campeón de goleo en España en 5 ocasiones.

Hugo Sánchez is shown here during a game against Norway in 1994.

Aquí vemos a Hugo Sánchez durante un partido contra Noruega en 1994.

In 2005, Mexico won the U-17 World Cup. Player Carlos Vela was named the best scorer in the cup after scoring five goals. Helping Vela was a group of talented players, which included César Villaluz, Ever Guzmán, and Giovani Dos Santos.

En 2005, México ganó la Copa del Mundo Sub-17. Además de Carlos Vela, que fue el líder de goleo en la copa con 5 anotaciones, México presentó a jugadores muy talentosos como César Villaluz, Ever Guzmán y Giovani Dos Santos.

Carlos Vela (right) helped Mexico win its first U-17 World Cup in 2005.

Carlos Vela (derecha) ayudó a México a ganar su primera Copa del Mundo Sub-17, en 2005.

The Mexican national team has a great future in soccer. Along with the U-17 champions, other young players, such as Guillermo Ochoa, Andrés Guardado, and Neri Castillo, are ready to give Mexican fans many more wins. The Mexican team will continue to make their place in soccer history.

México tiene un gran futuro por delante. Además de los campeones Sub-17, otros jóvenes jugadores como Guillermo Ochoa, Andrés Guardado y Neri Castillo parecen estar listos para darle a los aficionados mexicanos muchas victorias más.

MÉXICO

deration
927

── de Fútbol
   1927

	Home		Away
	Local		Visitante

hlights / Jugadores destacados

p Scorer / Mejor anotador   Best Player / Mejor jugador

Jared Borgetti (1997–)
46 goals / 46 goles

Hugo Sánchez (1977–1998)
75 caps / 75 convocatorias
29 goals / 29 goles

eam

ghlights / Palmarés del equipo

CONCACAF Championship /
Campeonato de CONCACAF
   Winner / Ganador: 1965, 1971
   Runner-Up / Segundo: 1967

CONCACAF Gold Cup / Copa de Oro CONCACAF
   Winner / Ganador: 1993, 1996, 1998, 2003
   Runner-Up / Segundo: 2007

FIFA U-17 World Cup / Copa Mundial FIFA Sub-17
   Winner / Ganador: 2005

GLOSSARY / GLOSARIO

defender (dih-FEND-er) A player who tries to keep the other team from scoring a goal.

exciting (ik-SY-ting) Interesting.

tournament (TOR-nuh-ment) A group of games that decides the best team.

World Cup (WUR-uld KUP) A group of games that takes place every four years with teams from around the world.

Copa del Mundo (la) Competencia de fútbol, cada 4 años, en la que juegan los mejores equipos del mundo.

defensa Un jugador que evita que el otro equipo anote goles.

emocionante Muy interesante.

torneo (el) Un grupo de partidos que deciden cuál es el mejor equipo.

RESOURCES / RECURSOS

Books in English / Libros en inglés

Gifford, Clive. *The Kingfisher Soccer Encyclopedia*. Boston: Kingfisher, 2006.

Shea, Therese. *Soccer Stars*. New York: Children's Press, 2006.

Books in Spanish / Libros en español

Contró, Arturo. *Rafael Márquez*. New York: PowerKids Press/Editorial Buenas Letras, 2008.

Dann, Sarah. *Fútbol en acción (Soccer in Action)*. New York: Crabtree Publishing, 2005.

Web Sites

Due to the changing nature of Internet links, PowerKids Press has developed an online list of Web sites related to the subject of this book. This site is updated regularly. Please use this link to access the list:
www.powerkidslinks.com/soct/mexico/

INDEX

ÍNDICE